D1302787

WORLD OF INSECTS

Butterflies

by Martha E. H. Rustad

BELLWETHER MEDIA · MINNEAPOLIS, MN

Note to Librarians, Teachers, and Parents:

Blastoff! Readers are carefully developed by literacy experts and combine standards-based content with developmentally-appropriate text.

Level 1 provides the most support through repetition of high-frequency words, light text, predictable sentence patterns, and strong visual support.

Level 2 offers early readers a bit more challenge through varied simple sentences, increased text load, and less repetition of high frequency words.

Level 3 advances early-fluent readers toward fluency through increased text and concept load, less reliance on visuals, longer sentences, and more literary language.

Level 4 builds reading stamina by providing more text per page, increased use of punctuation, greater variation in sentence patterns, and increasingly challenging vocabulary.

Level 5 encourages children to move from "learning to read" to "reading to learn" by providing even more text, varied writing styles, and less familiar topics.

Whichever book is right for your reader, Blastoff! Readers are the perfect books to build confidence and encourage a love of reading that will last a lifetime!

This edition first published in 2008 by Bellwether Media.

No part of this publication may be reproduced in whole or in part without written permission of the publisher. For information regarding permission, write to Bellwether Media Inc., Attention: Permissions Department, Post Office Box 1C, Minnetonka, MN 55345-9998.

Library of Congress Cataloging-in-Publication Data
Rustad, Martha E. H. (Martha Elizabeth Hillman), 1975–
  Butterflies / by Martha E. H. Rustad.
    p. cm. — (Blastoff! readers. World of insects)
Summary: "Simple text accompanied by full-color photographs give an upclose look at butterflies. Intended for kindergarten through third grade students"–Provided by publisher.
  Includes bibliographical references and index.
  ISBN-13: 978-1-60014-075-4 (hardcover : alk. paper)
  ISBN-10: 1-60014-075-0 (hardcover : alk. paper)
  1. Butterflies–Juvenile literature. I. Title.

  QL544.2.R87 2008
  595.78'9–dc22   2007007467

Contents

Butterflies are **insects**.

Butterflies hatch from eggs. They begin life as **caterpillars**.

Caterpillars eat leaves all day long. They grow quickly.

Caterpillars outgrow their skin and **shed** it many times.

A full-grown caterpillar forms a shell around its body. It is called a **chrysalis**.

Its body changes inside the chrysalis. The caterpillar becomes a butterfly.

Soon the butterfly pushes
out of the chrysalis.

It waits for its wet wings to dry. Then it can fly.

Butterflies have a narrow
body and four wings.

Tiny colored **scales** cover each wing. They form **patterns**.

Some butterflies are brown
or gray. They can look
like leaves.

Some butterflies have bright colors. Bright colors show birds a butterfly is bad to eat.

Butterflies eat **nectar** from flowers. Nectar gives them energy for flying.

antennas

Butterflies use their **antennas** to smell. This is how they find nectar.

17

All insects have six legs.
Butterflies can taste nectar
with the tips of their legs.

mouth

Butterflies have a mouth shaped like a straw. They drink nectar through it.

Butterflies lay eggs on leaves. They make a sticky liquid that holds the eggs to the leaves.

Soon new caterpillars
will hatch from the eggs.

Glossary

antennas—a pair of long and thin feelers on an insect's head; butterflies use their antennas to find food.

caterpillar—a young butterfly that looks like a worm; this form of a butterfly is also called a larva.

chrysalis—a hard shell that forms around a caterpillar as it changes into a butterfly

insect—a kind of animal with six legs; most insects also have a hard body, two antennas, and two or four wings.

nectar—sweet juice made by flowers

patterns—repeated colors and shapes

scale—a tiny colored plate on the wing of a butterfly

shed—to take off

To Learn More

AT THE LIBRARY

Barnard, Edward S. *Butterflies*. Pleasantville, N.Y.: Reader's Digest Young Families, 2006.

Carle, Eric. *The Very Hungry Caterpillar*. New York: Philomel Books, 1994.

Cooper, Jason. *Butterflies*. Vero Beach, Fla.: Rourke, 2006.

Rabe, Tish. *My, Oh My—A Butterfly!: All about Butterflies*. New York: Random House, 2007.

Stewart, Melissa. *Butterflies*. Minnetonka, Minn.: NorthWord Books for Young Readers, 2007.

ON THE WEB

Learning more about butterflies is as easy as 1, 2, 3.

1. Go to www.factsurfer.com

2. Enter "butterflies" into search box.

3. Click the "Surf" button and you will see a list of related web sites.

With factsurfer.com, finding more information is just a click away.

Index

The photographs in this book are reproduced through the courtesy of: Cathy Keifer, front cover, pp. 10-11, 15; Geoff Du Feu/Getty Images, p. 4; Robert Pickett/Alamy, pp. 5, 20; Don Johnston/Alamy, pp. 6, 8; Gary Meszaros/Getty Images, p. 7; Art Wolfe/Getty Images, p. 9; Shironina Lidiya Alexandrvna, p. 12; Sandra Caldwell, p. 13; Hwang Soo Pingp. 14; altrendo nature/Getty Images, p. 16; Gail Shumway/Getty Images, p. 17; Le-dung Ly/Getty Images, p. 18, Nic Hamilton/Alamy, p. 19; Robert Darrington/Alamy, p. 21.